# Where Did They Go?

Alexandra Behr

A Haights Cross Communications Company

A Haights Cross Communications Company

Published by
Sundance Publishing
P.O. Box 740
One Beeman Road
Northborough, MA 01532-0740
800-343-8204
www.sundancepub.com

*Where Did They Go?*
ISBN 0-7608-9358-6

Illustrations by Tony Griego

Photo Credits
cover (background) ©Guy Motil/CORBIS, (ship) Courtesy of the Naval Historical
Center; p. 1 ©Ted Spiegel/CORBIS; p. 6 ©Bettmann/CORBIS; pp. 6–7 ©Warren
Faidley/Weatherstock; p. 7 (plane) ©Bettmann/CORBIS, (globe) Larry Williams/CORBIS;
pp. 8–9 ©Galen Rowell/CORBIS; p. 9 ©Hulton-Deutsch Collection/CORBIS; p. 10–11
(ship) Courtesy of the Naval Historical Center, (wave) ©Steve Wilkings/CORBIS; p. 11
Courtesy of the Naval Historical Center; p. 12 Courtesy of the Federal Bureau of
Investigation; pp. 12–13 ©Bill Ross/CORBIS; p.16 ©Layne Kennedy/CORBIS; p.17
©Reuters/CORBIS; pp. 18–19 ©Robert Holmes/CORBIS; p. 19 ©Kevin Fleming/CORBIS;
p. 20–21 ©Danny Lehman/CORBIS; p. 21©Bettmann/CORBIS; pp. 24–25 ©Tom
Bean/CORBIS; pp. 26–27 ©Ted Spiegel/CORBIS; p. 28 Kislak Collection at the Library
of Congress; p. 29 Courtesy of the Lost Colony Waterside Theatre on Roanoke
Island, Manteo, NC; back cover (left) ©Bettmann/CORBIS, (right) Courtesy of the
Lost Colony Waterside Theatre on Roanoke Island, Manteo, NC

Printed in Canada

# Table
## of Contents

# Disappearing Acts

## Abracadabra, they're gone!

Some people have become famous—or more famous—by disappearing without a trace. No one can say for sure what really happened to them. They're just . . . gone!

Abracadabra!

# A Final Flight

Amelia Earhart's voice crackled over the radio, "Fuel is running low...." It was 1937. Amelia was supposed to become the first woman to fly around the world. But something was going wrong.

Amelia and her **navigator** had already flown 22,000 miles. On the morning of July 2, they had taken off from an island in the Pacific Ocean, with 7,000 dangerous miles to go.

But after sending her final message, Amelia's plane disappeared somewhere over the Pacific. The plane and its passengers were never found.

Amelia Earhart

# Flying Then and Now

| In 1937 | Now |
|---|---|
| • Smaller, slower planes with less fuel | • Bigger, faster jet planes |
| • Wireless radio limited to short distances | • Satellites allowing radio contact anywhere on earth |
| • New radar not effective | • Computer-guided planes, using advanced radar |

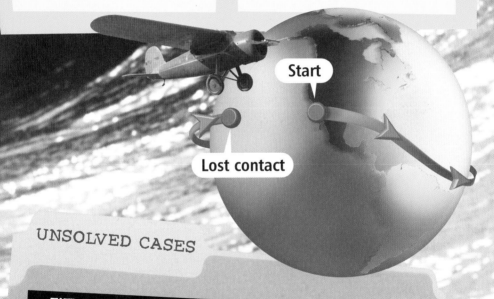

Start

Lost contact

UNSOLVED CASES

## What Happened to Amelia?

Some people think that . . .

> Earhart and her navigator got lost and ran out of fuel.

> Earhart was an American spy who got captured by the Japanese.

> Earhart's plane crashed on one of the small islands in the Pacific.

# Mega Mountain Mystery

Mount Everest is the highest spot on Earth. As of 1924, no one had ever reached the top.

That year on June 8, George Mallory and Sandy Irvine were a day's hike from the top. From far away, another climber had spotted the men around noon. It was the last time they were seen alive.

For 75 years, no one knew the climbers' **fate**. Then, in 1999, Mallory's frozen body was found. But Irvine's body is still missing. So the mystery remains. Did Mallory and Irvine get to the top before they died?

Top of Mt. Everest

Irvine    Mallory

The brochure didn't say anything about this!

## Death Zone

Climbers call the top of Mt. Everest the Death Zone. Why?
- not enough oxygen
- below-zero temperatures
- sudden storms
- deadly avalanches

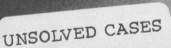

UNSOLVED CASES

## Did Mallory Make It?

Some people think that . . .

> Mallory and Irvine died before they reached the top.

> Mallory made it to the top because the photo of his wife he'd planned to leave at the top was not on his body in 1999.

9

# The *Cyclops* Is Gone!

The *Cyclops* was one of the biggest ships in the U.S. Navy. It was so big, it needed a crew of nearly 300 men.

In 1918, the *Cyclops* was steaming for Baltimore. But somewhere in the Caribbean Sea, the ship and its crew vanished. The Navy searched for months for the ship. They found no signs of the wreck or crew. The fate of the *Cyclops* is still one of the great mysteries of Navy history.

Uh-oh.

## What Happened to the *Cyclops*?

Some people think that...

> The ship ran into a gigantic, rogue wave.

> An enemy torpedo sank the ship.

> A sea ceature brought it down.

**Sailor on *Cyclops***

## Rogue Waves

These giant waves come out of nowhere—and with no warning. They can be as high as a ten-story building. They can even sink ocean liners. The scariest part is that scientists don't really know what causes them!

# Take the Money and Jump

The airplane sat on a rainy Seattle runway. Inside, a **hijacker** named D. B. Cooper tied a bag around his waist. It was filled with $200,000 in **ransom**. He had just set free all of the passengers. Then he strapped two parachutes to his body and ordered the pilot to take off. The year was 1971.

WANTED!!!

D. B. Cooper in 1971, and how he might look now

I guess crime really doesn't pay. . . .

The plane flew low over a Washington forest. Cooper opened the plane door. He jumped into the dark, rainy night.

Police searched the forest for months. There were no signs of Cooper. Nine years later, a boy came across $6,000 of ransom money. It's the only clue ever found.

UNSOLVED CASES

## Where Did Cooper Go?

Some people think that . . .

> Cooper was not prepared to live in the woods, so he died there.

> A Florida man named Duane Weber may have been Cooper. He told his wife he was Cooper just before he died. That claim has not been proved or disproved.

# Hide Your Valuables!

## A room of sparkling jewels! Paintings worth millions! Buried treasure!

They're all missing! Where did they go?
They didn't just walk off on their own.
Sometimes valuable things are taken and
never seen again.

# Royal Room Robbery?

The Amber Room was called the Eighth Wonder of the World. Its walls were covered with amber, gold, and gems. A German king had the room made in 1716 as a gift for the ruler of Russia.

Today the room would be worth more than $142 million! That is, if we could find it.

In World War II, invading Germans stole the walls of the Amber Room. After the war, Russia demanded them back. But no one could find them. The Amber Room was gone!

## What Is Amber?

Amber is a gold-colored substance used to make jewelry and to decorate. But it is not a gem. Amber is actually tree sap from prehistoric times.

My brother was stolen from the Amber Room!

A spider trapped in amber

A re-creation of the Amber Room

UNSOLVED CASES

## Where Did the Amber Room Go?

Some people think that . . .

> The walls of the Amber Room were burned in a fire.

> The walls were hidden in a silver mine in Germany.

# Cops As Robbers?

One winter night in 1990, two policemen knocked on a side door of the Isabella Stewart Gardner Museum in Boston. Little did the museum guards know that these men were crooks dressed as cops!

The phony cops tied up the guards. Then they stole as much as $500 million worth of art. They even cut famous paintings from their frames! It was the biggest art **heist** in U.S. history. The saddest part for art lovers is that the case remains unsolved.

Knock, knock...

Q: Who's there?
A: Hans.

Q: Hans who?
A: Hans off the painting!

Museum courtyard

Rembrandt self-portrait

UNSOLVED CASES

## Who Took the Art?

Some people think that . . .

> An Irish terrorist group stole the artwork to sell for money.

> A man in prison planned the robbery. He has yet to confess.

19

# Panama's Lost Loot

Panama City was the richest city in the Americas. That made it a likely target for the world's most famous pirate, Henry Morgan. In 1671, Morgan gathered 2,000 other pirates on ships and sailed for Panama. His plan was to loot the city and steal its huge treasure.

But city leaders were ready. They had 700 tons of gold and jewels loaded onto three ships that sailed to a secret location.

Morgan didn't get his treasure. No one else did either. To this day, no one knows where the ships went.

UNSOLVED CASES

## Where Is the Treasure?

Some people think that...

> The treasure was buried in the hills of Costa Rica.

> A map existed to the treasure, but the map was destroyed.

20

Panama City ruins

21

# Mystery in the Ruins?

## A few people missing is one thing. But a whole town of people?

How could big groups of people disappear without a trace? It seems impossible. But it has happened—more than once.

# Missing Civilization

In our Southwest, ancient cliff-side homes sit empty in desert canyons. They were built 2,000 years ago by the Anasazi people. Now those people are gone.

About 30,000 Anasazi developed a great **civilization** in the harsh desert. It lasted for centuries. Then almost suddenly, in about 1300, the Anasazi were gone.

How could a whole civilization disappear? To this day, we still don't know for sure.

Whew, it's hot! No wonder they left!

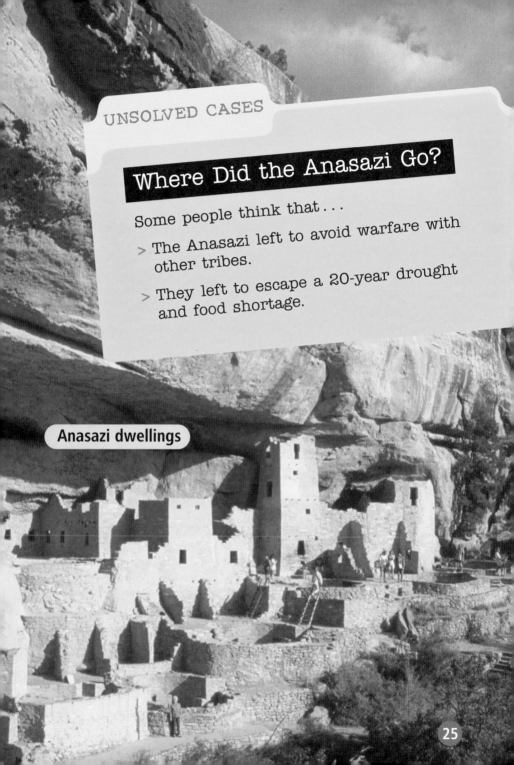

## Where Did the Anasazi Go?

Some people think that...

> The Anasazi left to avoid warfare with other tribes.

> They left to escape a 20-year drought and food shortage.

Anasazi dwellings

# Vanished Vikings

Move over, Christopher Columbus. The Vikings beat you to North America.

In 986, a small group of Vikings arrived in Greenland. They found a cold, harsh land. Still, for hundreds of years they **prospered** in stone villages along the coast.

But by 1721, the Vikings of Greenland were gone. No one knows where they went. Only the ruins of 400 buildings remained.

Well, guys, it's definitely not Florida!

**Viking longboat**

## Little Green Lie

A Viking named Eric the Red thought he could get settlers from Iceland to move to a nearby island he'd found. He named it Greenland. He said it was very green and fertile. But that was a lie! It turned out to be mostly covered by a sheet of ice.

UNSOLVED CASES

## Where Did the Vikings Go?

Some people think that...

> Greenland got too cold and the Vikings died off.

> The Vikings became cut off from Europe and did not have supplies they needed to survive.

# Lost Virginia Colony

After three years away, John White could not wait to return to Roanoke Island. With help from local Indian people, he and others had started a colony there in 1587. But when White returned, not one of the 103 settlers was in sight. Everyone was gone!

White found the name of a nearby island carved into a fence. But the settlers were not there either. The lost colony of Roanoke remains a mystery.

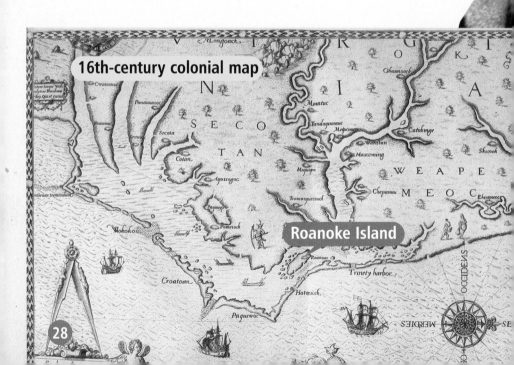

16th-century colonial map

Roanoke Island

Actors in clothing of the times

Help! This corset is killing me!

## UNSOLVED CASES

## A Whole Colony Lost?

Some people think that . . .

> Some hostile Indian people killed the Roanoke settlers.

> Suffering from the worst drought in 800 years, the Roanoke settlers moved away.

29

# Fact File

Costa Ricans are certain the Panama treasure is buried in Costa Rica. They say that the metal ruins TV reception there!

The Vikings buried dead warriors in longboats surrounded by treasure.

The world's most stolen painting is *Jacob III de Gheyn* by Rembrandt. It has been snatched 4 times in the last 35 years.

So this is the New World....

Among the lost Roanoke settlers was the first English child born in America—Virginia Dare.

# Glossary

**civilization**  the way that a group of people lives at a certain time in history

**fate**  a final outcome

**heist**  a robbery

**hijacker**  a person who takes control of an airplane by force or the threat of force

**navigator**  a person who plans the route for an airplane or a ship

**prospered**  lived successfully

**ransom**  money demanded by a criminal in exchange for the release of a hostage

# Index